EMPIRE STYLE

Translated from the French by Emily Lane

First published in Great Britain in 1999 by
Thames and Hudson Ltd, London

British Library Cataloguing-in-Publication Data
A catalogue record for this book is available from the British Library

ISBN 0-500-01968-1

Printed and bound in Italy

EMPIRE STYLE

François Baudot

Thames & Hudson

The Empire style in history

Since the Renaissance, every French style has taken its name, more or less aptly, from that of a French king: the Americans call it all 'the Louis'. Empire, on the other hand, does not just mean the style of Napoleon I: the term tries to denote something larger, less circumscribed, more international, something like a break or a sudden accident in the history of taste. It is possible to inherit or acquire the most disparate pieces of furniture and live with them happily, without a second thought. But Empire pieces must be consciously chosen, sought out, justified – one might almost say acquired by decree: at a casual glance, their ornamentation of Ns, bees and sphinxes might seem absurd rather than admirable.

In Proust's *À la Recherche du temps perdu*, when the Duchesse de Guermantes is finally converted by Swann and Charlus to the merits of this all-conquering style and decides to have the imperial pieces of furniture that her husband had inherited brought down from the attics, she is careful to make her decision look like a mere whim. To the natural heirs of the Enlightenment in France, Empire always suggested officialdom or the *nouveau riche* – at best the world of the diplomat, at worst that of the civil servant. Welcomed by a few historically minded specialists, tolerated by senior civil servants, a standard background to career officials, these heavy pieces, long regarded as funereal, seemed designed for official ceremonies rather than intimate gatherings, for proclamations rather than private gossip.

Closer to the spirit of republican Rome than to that of republican Athens, this style focused on antiquity is monumental even in its most domestic manifestations. Its motifs come from architecture, and no other style is so perfectly integrated into its architectural setting. The difficulty of placing Empire pieces in an alien context was brilliantly tackled in the twentieth century, especially by interior designers between the wars, who played witty games with all aspects of Neoclassicism. Empire nonetheless remains an uncompromising, absolute style, a style of ensembles. It is the first French style to remind one of the world of design as we know it today – a style whose practitioners were equally adept at cutlery and façades, at the detailing of a frieze and of a chair, at the plan of a fortress and the shape of a gown to be worn at court.

Every period of history has seen a gradual evolution of the styles of façades, interiors, and furniture, in response to the needs of the time. Contraries, contrasts and contradictions have coexisted, especially in country areas. Empire, on the other hand – an essentially urban manner – came into being as a unit, decreed by a small group of people, almost at a stroke. Standing on the threshold of a new century full of promise, turning its back on the past, fashion surrendered, and hastily decorated the old walls with eagles, victories, and laurel crowns many of which survive to the present day – at Versailles, at the Louvre, even at the Invalides, where it is easy to forget that the gilded dome dates from the time of the Sun King, not the Emperor. Napoleon, all-conquering as he was, built relatively little, as war occupied first his time and then his state's finances, and the glory of absolutism was most characteristically reflected through ornament, interior decoration, and the development of industries producing luxury goods.

What mattered above all was to stage-manage the pageantry of empire by adjusting the customs of the Ancien Régime to a world in political and social turmoil, as Europe was conquered by men of high courage but for the most part of modest background. The freshly gilded interiors of old *hôtels*, refurbished for the laurel-crowned heroes of Year II, gave a totalitarian, self-made-man connotation to the Empire style that it has still not entirely shaken off in its homeland. Napoleon was unaware of such subtleties. He had himself clearly set out the principles that art was to follow in the service of his absolute rule, writing in 1805 to Intendant-Général Daru: 'My aim is to make the arts address subjects that will keep alive the memory of the achievements of the past fifteen years.' A few men of genius, a few brilliant designers, successfully realized that aim, carried along by the strong, austere current of Neoclassicism that had been swelling throughout Europe for a generation. As early as the 1750s, at the height of Rococo, the discovery of the ruins of Pompeii and the archaeological publications that ensued prompted a rediscovery of antique design. Purity of line, functionalism and simplicity became the order of the day, from the newborn United States to tsarist Russia, with many local variations but an overall consensus. Self-respecting young men, especially those who were both rich and English, felt honour-bound to make the 'Grand Tour' as a pilgrimage to see the classical remains in southern Europe. Passing through Enlightenment Paris and Voltaire's Switzerland, they went on to Venice, Rome, Naples, Capri or Syracuse. Against this wider international background Napoleon's France developed its own highly original style. The painter Jacques-Louis David and the architect Claude-Nicolas Ledoux had shown new paths to explore; but beyond that, it was the ancient Roman ideals of heroism, purity and civic virtue that inspired Napoleon, who had been 'consul' before proclaiming himself emperor.

I n 1784 David's *Oath of the Horatii* was unveiled, embodying the austere moral standards that were to characterize the Revolutionary bourgeoisie. The clarity of its composition, the simplicity of its forms and the austerity of its setting were ideals taken up by the archaeologist and politician Quatremère de Quincy in his *Dictionnaire de l'architecture* ('Dictionary of architecture', 1795–1825). The real foundation of the new imperial style, however, was the *Recueil de décorations intérieures* ('Collection of interior designs', 1801 and 1812) of Charles Percier and Pierre-François-Léonard Fontaine, with its strong reliance on the 'antique'. Napoleon was fond of using allusion to confirm the legitimacy of his rule, and for him Percier and Fontaine took up motifs from ancient history and adapted them to suit new purposes, a new scale, and new techniques.

Empire is a state of mind more than a style. Its span is the first fifteen years of the nineteenth century, emerging from the Directoire style of the late Revolutionary period and the Consulat style of the turn of the century. Afterwards, when Louis XVIII returned from his long exile, he hastily removed the most blatant imperial symbols before settling down in the usurper's furniture, a situation not without its irony. Charles X came to the throne in 1825: no aesthete himself, he handed over the role of fashion arbiter to Marie-Caroline of Naples, Duchesse de Berri. She herself encouraged an interest in the Gothic style, inspired by French translations of Scott, Goethe and Schiller, and then by the publication in 1831 of Victor Hugo's *Notre-Dame de Paris*. Neoclassicism, however, remained the official style: Percier and Fontaine, and the cabinetmaker Jacob-Desmalter, all retained their positions. Work went on on building projects of the Empire, such as the Palais Royal, the Madeleine, the Étoile and the Bourse, and the model of antiquity, with its marbles, its columns and its cornucopias, continued to shape the productions of architects such as Bélanger, Lecointe, Hittorff and Brongniart and painters such as Ingres, Devéria and Gros. There was, however, a move towards a more bourgeois, lighter-toned, more curvaceous aesthetic. The architect yielded supremacy to the decorator, and grandeur made way for comfort. There were already the first signs of the eclecticism that would clutter the rest of the nineteenth century with its invasive bric-a-brac.

a t the end of the century, it was a desire for greater simplicity and cohesion that led the aesthetes of Proust's time to rediscover Neoclassicism. Faced with the Third Republic, Ancien Régime aristocrats and the children of Empire grandees found common cause. It is also possible to see in the codified, easily reproducible vocabulary of Empire decoration a prefiguration of the standardization of design which the mass-production of consumer goods was beginning to impose. One of the more intriguing paradoxes of the Empire style is that it used modern mechanized production to promote antiquity. It is almost always hard to copy styles of the past without falling into disheartening pastiche, but imitation Empire can be produced by the metre: witness the enthusiasm with which it is taken up today for French ministry buildings, international 'palaces', and fashion design. The explanation lies in the fact that with its severe, straight lines and its modern ideas of functionalism, Empire belongs to the incipient industrial age. Before the nineteenth century, objects and forms were devised by a craftsman, working more or less on his own; thereafter, they increasingly depended on designs or ideas handed down from above – from official bodies, from the laboratories of fashion, from studios – even though the concept of industrial design had yet to be thought up. The chairs available as standard products from Jacob are the ancestors of the mass-produced chairs of today.

Neoclassicism

I n 1774, at the beginning of the reign of Louis XVI, when the world was about to embark on more than a quarter-century of upheaval, there was a feeling in France that the rules that governed society were in need of complete revision. Nobility, clergy and gentry, the economy and even the arts, everything was thrown open to debate, and there were schemes for major reforms. Many of the changes initiated at the time shaped the world as we know it today. In the visual realm, reform took the shape of a return to the primitive beauty of antiquity, a move inaugurated by Jacques-Ange Gabriel with the building of the Petit Trianon at Versailles in 1762–68. Also in the late eighteenth century, the Grande Galerie of the Louvre was cleared to create the first French 'museum'. In 1794, Alexandre Lenoir began planning a large 'Musée des Monuments Français', prompted by the extensive destruction of buildings and art works during the Revolution. René de Chateaubriand wrote *Le*

Génie du christianisme (1802) and then *Les Martyrs* (1809). Hubert Robert painted compositions of melancholy ruins. New gardens were laid out in English style, dotted with Altars of Friendship, Temples of Reason, urns, hermitages and little buildings inspired by ancient structures in Greece and Sicily.

b y the end of the eighteenth century decoration was characterized by linear forms, right angles and plain surfaces, with a minimum of decoration on borders alone, in the form of palmettes, garlands, egg-and-dart, beading, dentils and Greek key. Lions, chimeras, griffins and sphinxes (already) provided models for bronze-castings, sculptures, and thousands of architectural carvings. Furniture too had become more rectilinear and looked to Greece and Rome for its vocabulary, with a profusion of columns, of fluting, of wheatsheaves, wreaths and lyres, of motifs derived from 'Etruscan' (i.e. Greek) vases, of X-frame bases and of backs with angular openwork decoration. The late Louis XVI and Directoire periods were dominated by the family of Georges Jacob (1739–1814), a chair-maker with a great range of patterns in solid or veneered mahogany, their sober orthogonal shapes decorated with bronze and coloured inlay. His sons, Georges II (1768–1803) and François-Honoré (1770–1841), succeeded him and transformed his workshop into a firm. Under the name 'Jacob-Desmalter' it became the chief supplier to the Emperor, working mainly to designs by Percier and Fontaine. After the Hundred Days, at the Restoration the firm received commissions for the Palais de l'Élysée, home of the Duc de Berry.

the makers of textiles and block-printed wallpapers did not lag behind, taking their subjects from the loves of the gods, the story of Psyche, and Pompeian decorative schemes. Medallions and cameos mingled with mythological scenes, volutes and rinceaux with architectural arabesques derived from Italy. Manufactures such as that founded by Christophe-Philippe Oberkampf in 1759 at Jouy-en-Josas, where the celebrated printed cottons still popular today as 'toile de Jouy' were originally made, are significant not just for the charm of their products but for their role as precursors of the factories that were to multiply in the following century. In that context, it is significant that the first social strife at the start of the Revolution broke out in the Réveillon works in the Faubourg Saint-Antoine, which was famous for its block-printed papers available in standard designs. Silversmiths were already using motifs from antiquity before the death of Louis XV; their search for purity of form was accompanied by a turning away from traditional techniques in favour of casting, which was less fine but more profitable, and the use of separate decorative motifs applied cold by means of screws and bolts. Here too, before the advent of Napoleon, we find a foreshadowing of the great industrial expansion that was to occur in France in the 1850s. In 1771 Joseph Cugnot, an engineer in Lorraine, invented a steam-powered freight-carrier – the first of all those 'horse-powered' automobiles that have followed on behind the chariots of the gods.

The Directoire

●

Initiated in August 1795 by the Constitution of Year III, the Directoire presided over the worsening economic, financial and social crisis that followed the fall of the Ancien Régime. Speculation was rife, and among the rich many enjoyed a worldly, libertine life. This period of intense contrasts was brought to an end by Napoleon's coup d'état of 18 Brumaire Year VIII (9 November 1799). Though short, the Directoire left its mark, and its name still evokes a world of stylish, unprincipled freedom – best exemplified, perhaps, in female fashion, with its sensuous, unrestricted forms, as stiff corsets, panniers and trains gave way to the fluid silhouette of transparent fabrics draped in Grecian shapes. To summon up this period of transition, one need only think of portraits of Madame Récamier or Josephine de Beauharnais. In the decorative arts, 'Directoire' is to 'Empire' as 'Bonaparte' is to 'Napoleon' – the freshest, most enthusiastic, most elegant aspect of an age of restless turmoil.

In architecture, the new manner and the visionary projects of Boullée, Ledoux and Lequeu attracted a following. Celebrations were held in honour of the Supreme Being or the goddess Reason. Soufflot's church of Sainte-Geneviève in Paris was transformed into a 'Pantheon' under the supervision of Quatremère de Quincy. The painter David designed settings for celebrations, costumes for great occasions, and furniture, full of allusions to Roman legions, to the heroic conduct of the Spartan king Leonidas, and to the ancient world depicted in the pages of Plutarch. Interior decoration took on the relaxed grace and colours of Pompeii and Herculaneum before the catastrophe of Vesuvius – shades of terracotta, vines, pergolas, birds, lilacs, bacchantes, harmonies of pale tones, single-coloured panels edged by thin borders, ceilings decorated with parasol shapes, medallion-filled friezes, trompe-l'oeil oculi, *faux* stone, *faux* bronze and *faux* marble. In this brief golden age of decoration, gods became human, draperies became ethereal spiders' webs, and chairs took on the X-frame shape that Julius Caesar sat on.

Often revived in later years, the Directoire style stands in stark contrast to the savagery of its time. In furniture it took the forms evolved under Louis XVI and added a profusion of lozenges, vases, griffes and hieroglyphs, straighter lines, stripes, and metal trimmings. Seats and beds looked to the military camp. Jardinières turned into *athéniennes* (delicate stands supporting bowls, named from a popular painting by Vien called *The Virtuous Athenian Lady*). You couldn't have a straightforward vase: it had to be a perfume-burner. Softwoods were painted in light colours, but the spirit of the age was more truly reflected in manly mahogany. Yet manners grew more frivolous and dresses more transparent, as with Mars and Venus spurs entered the boudoir; Cupids painted on the canopies of beds discreetly shut their eyes...

Empire

the Empire style begins with 'Consulat', the name applied by antique dealers to some of the most beautiful Napoleonic furniture, notably that made by the ébéniste Bernard Molitor. At this stage, the cult of the hero was still subsumed to the influence of antiquity, the worldly elegance of Josephine de Beauharnais, and the philosophy of the Enlightenment. A new type of bed was invented, in the shape known as 'en gondole' (gondola-like): with two symmetrical curved ends, it was designed to stand lengthwise against a wall or in an alcove. The gilded decorations that thickly encrust the Cuban mahogany were delicately chiselled, light and fantastical. Imperial dignity would soon require them to be stiffer, more formal, and more uniform, replacing Etruscan-style grotesque decoration by eagles, bees, swans, monograms, and all the panoply of authority. Concerned with display and with fostering the production of luxury goods, Napoleon encouraged his followers to use rich textiles; chief among these were silks, of which the manufacture in Lyons was brilliantly relaunched, chiefly by the workshops of Camille Pernon and later the Grand brothers. Crucial to this process was the perfection by Joseph-Marie Jacquard of the loom that bears his name, which gave an immense impetus to the production of sumptuous damasks and brocades. For everything from curtains to ladies' trains, such textiles became indispensable. The men who accompanied those ladies, from Bonaparte on down, shone with new titles assumed from conquered towns, captive provinces and subject states.

t he château of Malmaison was Josephine's personal property; here Napoleon liked to live and work in the early years of their marriage. It survives with its interiors, its gardens and its air of informality to give us a perfect impression of the mood of enthusiasm that surrounded the birth of the Empire – perhaps because here the influence was that of a sensitive woman as well as of a Promethean genius.

At the heart of power, ensconced in his palaces, Napoleon had leisure to develop suitable imagery for his living legend. In this a major role was played, albeit behind the scenes, by the distinctive, engaging figure of Dominique Vivant Denon (1747–1825). Denon was already fifty-one when in 1798 he met Napoleon in Josephine's *salon* and persuaded the

Consul to allow him to go to Egypt with the army that was embarking at Toulon. He was a typical man of the Enlightenment, courteous, eloquent, cultivated and sophisticated, and had already served on several diplomatic missions. More than ten years spent in Rome had sharpened his sense of curiosity, especially for matters archaeological. During the Revolution he had kept a low profile. He now set out for Egypt with General Desaix's division full of enthusiasm, though there was as yet nothing to suggest the great consequences that his self-assigned mission would have. As soon as he landed in Alexandria, on 3 July 1798, Denon began sketching, copying, measuring, tracing and recording everything and anything that came the soldiers' way. With the material that he accumulated during his thirteen-month stay he compiled his epoch-making *Voyage dans la Basse et Haute Égypte pendant les campagnes du général Bonaparte* ('Travels in Lower and Upper Egypt during the campaigns of General Bonaparte'), the title in itself serving clearly as a political dedication. Its publication in 1802 had an electrifying effect throughout Europe: here suddenly was something quite different from the classical culture inherited from ancient Greece – a civilization that was even older, and much more mysterious. It was the beginning of a close, distinctive, and lasting relationship between the banks of the Seine and the banks of the Nile. Central to the influence of the *Voyage* was Denon's novel idea of giving illustrations as much space as text: the plates volume, with its appealing and meticulous images and its full captions, could almost be seen as an ancestor of the picture-guide.

Here, Bonaparte saw immediately, was the means by which a military failure could be transformed into something of epic status. Through Denon the general became a patron of learning and aesthetics, and Denon was accordingly appointed director of a central 'muséum'. In that capacity he reigned over the arts, constructing a new relationship between them and politics: in a way that prefigures modern practice, he became an image-maker, promoting Egyptian fashions to associate the new world-ruler, who had seized power through a coup d'état, with the prestigious ancient pharaohs, and with an exotic expedition that had greatly widened the horizons of European imagination. Denon's great mission was achieved through many small means, as contemporary design worked to propagate the myth. Jacob-Desmalter created Egyptian-style furniture, Sèvres produced a sensational table service in biscuit porcelain, clocks took on the form of Egyptian pylons, modest doors became temple gateways. Countless fountains, monuments, chairs, andirons, candelabra, and even panoramic wallpapers carried the message of this radically new adventure throughout Europe.

all Europe was soon looking at and copying what was happening in France, and the new interiors of the châteaux of Saint-Cloud, Compiègne and Fontainebleau, of the imperial apartments in the Tuileries, and of private houses like the Hôtel de Beauharnais in Paris (now the German Embassy) were reflected in designs that ranged from the cabinet of the King of Spain in the palace of Aranjuez to furniture in the antique manner designed by the English connoisseur Thomas Hope. With the exception of a few buildings celebrating the glory of the Empire, French domestic exteriors maintained late eighteenth-century forms; but their interior decoration became more and more architectural, to the point where small informal rooms took on the air of mausoleums. Doors were triumphal arches, walls aped peristyles, and chairs aspired to be thrones; desks looked like small fortresses, beds like tents, torches like trophies. A systematic, studied use of symmetry and repetition left less and less room for fantasy. White and gold, amaranth, imperial purple, all shades of red, emerald green and a great deal of mauve were the dominant tones in a dazzling range of colours, of which the splendour was further heightened by geometrically conceived embroidery, braid and incrustations. This world of canopic jars, lions, Horus falcons, and palm or lotus capitals was softened only by the equally strong passion for botany, which led to the welcome intrusion of flowers among the martial motifs.

good management of the conquered territories necessitated a multiplication of civil servants, and that in turn led Empire designers to play a pioneering role in the development of rational office furniture. In France the civil service grew until it was almost as powerful as it is today. It proved a short step from the Empire desk to the empire of the desk.

In *Les Employés* ('The Employees', 1836) Balzac describes the origin and growth of this 'tertiary' world, which soon acquired its own distinctive customs, landscape and equipment. Among its other effects, the rise of the bureaucracy meant an immense increase in the number of people sitting down. Before the fashion for the art of conversation and the *salon* developed in the eighteenth century, sitting down in company was not the norm that we take for granted today. The courtier and his lady spent most of their lives on their feet (or in bed); chairs were relatively rare, and first claim on them came from princes, the sick and the old. From now on, however, that seated posture would be increasingly enjoyed by civil servants. Is it perhaps a lingering association between Empire and stuffy bureaucracy that makes so many French people still dislike the style so intensely?

It would be quite wrong to associate what was a long and rich period of decorative art merely with chilly grandiloquence and absolute rule. As the nineteenth century wore on, the settings of the lives of those in power took on an increasingly bourgeois character that softened their initial arrogant grandeur. They remained, however, faithful to historical sources. There was none of the pastiche or eclectic imitation that characterize the mid and late nineteenth century. Not until Art Nouveau and modernism was there a return to such unity in ornament, interior decoration, furniture, and objects both beautiful and useful. While their early nineteenth-century settings may strike us today as somewhat daunting, removed from those settings many Empire pieces display true beauty and often a quite startling originality – that of a period that was determined to innovate, to simplify, to be rigorously logical; fired by noble ideals, it saw nothing wrong in expressing itself in the smallest details, right down to the tiniest button. Nothing could be too small in an age that thought big.

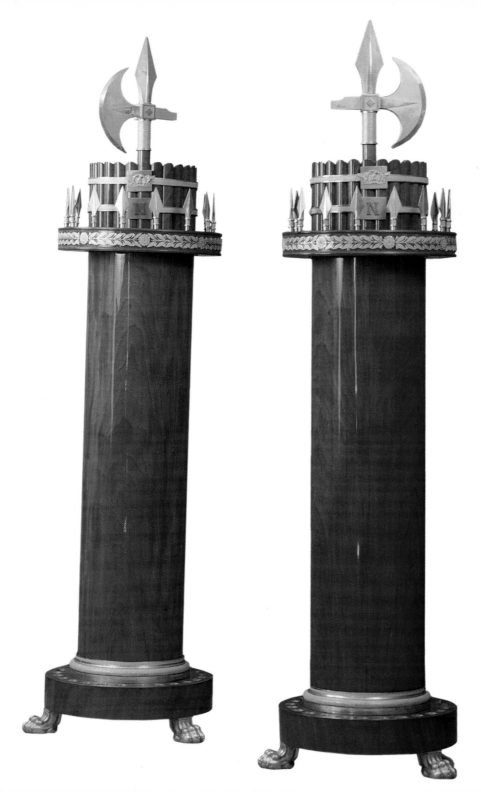

SALLE DES SAIZONS.

CAMPAGNE
EN EGYPTE

CAMPAGNE
EN ITALIE ET
EN ALLEMAGNE

Don Vauquier. Sept. 1935
Enr. n° 588.   n° 7

Chronology

1783   The firm of Christophe-Philippe Oberkampf, the main French producer of printed textiles, founded at Jouy-en-Josas in 1759, is awarded the title of royal manufactory; it was to grow significantly under the Directoire.

1784   *The Oath of the Horatii*, by David, introduces into painting the austere principles that the theoretical writings of Quatremère de Quincy transform into dogma.

1789   On 14 July, outbreak of the Revolution.

1791   Abolition of privileges. Traditional patronage dries up, under the combined effect of large-scale emigration and the nationalization of church property.

1793   Opening of the 'muséum', the forerunner of the Louvre, organized by Dominique Vivant Denon.
Closure of the academies, a deliberate attack on the traditional bodies that sought to maintain the fine craftsmanship of the eighteenth century.

1794   Creation of the Musée des Monuments Français by Alexandre Lenoir. This contributes to the gradual revaluation of the Middle Ages, which continues with the publication of Chateaubriand's *Génie du christianisme* (1802) and *Les Martyrs* (1809).

1795–97   Under the influence of the furniture designed for the Hôtel Montholon (1786, by Lequeu), for the painter David (1789), and for Madame Élisabeth (1790, by Brongniart and Dugourc), the 'Etruscan' style becomes fashionable for furniture and interior decoration: X-frame chairs, 'gondola' backs, etc.

1796–1803   In 1796, Josephine de Beauharnais marries Napoleon Bonaparte in a civil ceremony. She has Jacob Frères decorate and furnish her *hôtel* in the rue Chantereine in Paris. By now the cabinetmaker Georges Jacob, creator of David's furniture under the Revolution, has handed over his firm to his two sons, Georges and François-Honoré. Their fruitful partnership lasts until 1803. After the death of his elder brother, François-Honoré continues his prestigious career, under the name 'Jacob-Desmalter'.

1798   Napoleon leads a military expedition to Egypt with a large scientific contingent, which fuels an interest that had begun to emerge in the 1760s. Subsequently, encouraged by Vivant Denon and using motifs drawn from his engravings, the Manufacture de Sèvres produce many remarkable services.

1799   Napoleon is proclaimed First Consul by the Constitution of Year III.

1801   Charles Percier and Pierre-François-Léonard Fontaine, Napoleon's official architects and designers, publish their *Recueil de décorations intérieures*, republished in 1812, which is extremely influential in spreading the Empire style.

Château Margaux, in the Gironde, by Louis Combes:
a rare example of a country château in Neoclassical style.
© J.-P. Navicet/Explorer, Vanves.

1802	First Exhibition of the Products of Industry in Paris. A second is held in 1806. Publication by Dominique Vivant Denon of his *Voyage dans la Basse et Haute Égypte pendant les campagnes du général Bonaparte*. Designers and craftsmen draw on its illustrations, which are archaeologically extremely accurate.
1804	On 2 December, coronation of Napoleon in Notre Dame in Paris.
1804–14	Reign of Napoleon as Emperor. He initiates a systematic programme to refurnish the former royal residences. Great revival of the Lyons textile industries, helped by technical improvements introduced by Jacquard; the use of a new cylinder encourages the proliferation of patterns with many tiny motifs, and, after 1806, the imitation of cashmere designs. The reign is expressed architecturally in Paris with the façade of the Palais-Bourbon (1804–7), the Madeleine (1806), the Place de l'Étoile (begun 1806), and the Bourse (1808). Percier and Fontaine, seeking to give the new official style monumentality and grandeur, turn to a wide range of ideas from the past, reflected in interiors such as that of Napoleon's bedroom at Compiègne (1807). Martin-Guillaume Biennais, famous for his extremely refined work, is the Emperor's favourite silversmith; in his successful firm he has many assistants, including Jean-Charles Cahier, who succeeds him in 1819. The workshop of the bronze-worker Pierre-Philippe Thomire produces many candelabra and torchères of chill, refined design (e.g. for Napoleon's bedroom at Fontainebleau, 1810) and gives clocks a new monumentality (clock commemorating the Emperor's marriage, Compiègne).
1806	The epic story of Napoleon's wars is illustrated in the 378 bronze panels of the Column of the Grande Armée (Place Vendôme, Paris), cast from plaster models made by more than thirty sculptors to the designs of Pierre-Nicolas Bergeret.
1806–10	The Continental Blockade forces furniture-makers to turn to native woods (beech, oak, walnut, fruitwoods) or, for the interiors of courtiers' houses, to gilding.
1809–22	Publication of the monumental *Description de l'Égypte*, by the Commission des Sciences et des Arts of the Armée d'Orient – nine volumes of text and eleven of large-format plates, which, with Denon's earlier *Voyage*, lay the foundations of Egyptology.
1810–11	The dressing table of the Empress Marie-Louise (1810) and the cradle of the King of Rome (1811) made by Jean-Baptiste-Claude Odiot, the chief proponent of the massive style of the end of Napoleon's reign, with the assistance of P.-P. Prud'hon and P.-P. Thomire.
1815	Napoleon is defeated at Waterloo. His brother Joseph flees to America (to an estate at Point Breeze, New Jersey); this helps to spread the Empire style there, as do the products of the émigré cabinetmaker Charles-Honoré Lannuier and the silversmith Simon Chaudron.

X-frame stool from the Council Chamber in the Château of Saint-Cloud,
by Jacob Frères. Château de Malmaison. © Dagli Orti, Paris.

Empire Style

Columns with the cipher of Napoleon, by Pierre-Philippe Thomire. Mahogany and gilt bronze, H 217 cm, D 65 cm. These decorative columns served as stands for billiard cues. © Galerie Bernard Steinitz, Paris.
Napoleon visiting the New Staircase in the Louvre, under the Guidance of the Architects Percier and Fontaine, by Auguste Couder. Oil on canvas, 177.5 x 135 cm. Musée du Louvre, Paris. © AKG, Paris.

The Empress Marie-Louise and the King of Rome, by François Gérard, 1812. Musée Historique du Château, Versailles. © AKG, Paris.
Cradle of the King of Rome, designed by Pierre-Paul Prud'hon and made by Jean-Baptiste-Claude Odiot and Pierre-Philippe Thomire as a gift from the city of Paris, 1811. Silver gilt and mother of pearl. Kunsthistorisches Museum, Vienna. © AKG, Paris.

The Music Room, Malmaison, by Auguste Garneray (1785–1825). Watercolour. Château de Malmaison et de Bois-Préau. © Arnaudet/RMN, Paris.

Secretaire, by Jean-Baptiste Youf (1762–1838), 1830. 236 x 139 cm. Palazzo Pitti, Florence. © S. Domingie/M. Rabatti/AKG, Paris.
Armchair in the Music Room, Malmaison, by Jacob Frères. Mahogany and gilt bronze. Mahogany is also used for the columns and pilasters of the room. © Dagli Orti, Paris.

Napoleon's 'bureau mécanique', from the Emperor's study, by François-Honoré Jacob-Desmalter. Mahogany and gilt bronze. Château de Fontainebleau. © Lagiewski/RMN, Paris.

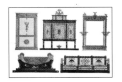

Plate 58 from the album *Meubles et objets de goût* by Pierre de La Mésangère (1802–35), showing a secretaire, dressing table, mirror/screen, bed with chimera terminals, and three-seater sofa of a type known as a 'paphos'. Bibliothèque des Arts Décoratifs, Paris. © Dagli Orti, Paris.

Napoleon's bedroom, Malmaison. © RMN, Paris.
Candelabrum and vase, attributed to Pierre-Philippe Thomire. Gilt bronze. Musée du Louvre, Paris. © RMN, Paris.

Athénienne, from Napoleon's bedroom in the Grand Trianon, Versailles, 1810. Mahogany, gilt bronze, and Sèvres porcelain, H 86 cm. Musée National du Château de Malmaison. © RMN, Paris. **Base of the Table of the Marshals** (detail), by Charles Percier, Jean-Baptiste Isabey and Pierre-Philippe Thomire, 1808–10. Gilt bronze and Sèvres porcelain. Porcelain was on rare occasions used for the tops or bases of tables. Château de Malmaison. © RMN, Paris.

Philibert Rivière, Maître des Requêtes in the King's Council, by Jean-Auguste-Dominique Ingres, 1815. Oil on canvas, 116 x 89 cm. Musée du Louvre, Paris. © Gérard Blot, RMN, Paris. **Salon Doré, Malmaison**: white and gold decoration of the ceiling and doors commissioned by Josephine in 1811; carved giltwood chairs; gilt bronze gueridon; clock of gilt bronze, malachite, and coloured stones, by Pierre-Philippe Thomire and Bourdier. © RMN, Paris.

Directoire armchair, attributed to Jacob Frères. Mahogany, 95 x 63 x 43 cm. © Laurent-Sully Jaulmes/Musée des Arts Décoratifs, Paris.
Napoleon's library, Malmaison, decorated by Charles Percier and Pierre-François-Léonard Fontaine in 1800. Wooden panelling, bookcases and desk by Jacob Frères. © Dagli Orti, Paris.

Chair 'en gondole', c. 1811. Mahogany. Château de Compiègne. © RMN, Paris.
Armchair, by François-Honoré Jacob-Desmalter. Mahogany. Château de Fontainebleau. © RMN, Paris.

The Salle des Saisons in the Louvre in 1802–3, by Hubert Robert. Oil on canvas, 37 x 46 cm. Musée du Louvre, Paris. © C. Jean/RMN, Paris.

Minerva, with a clock as her shield. Bronze with gilt details. Château de Malmaison. © RMN, Paris.
Large vase on stand with Egyptian motifs from the Tuileries Palace, Paris, by Debret. Painted sheet metal and gilt bronze. Musée du Louvre, Paris. © RMN, Paris.

Tripod, 1815. Villa Imperiale, Poggio a Caiano. © S. Domingie/M. Rabatti/ AKG, Paris.
State bedroom of the Empress Josephine, Malmaison, redecorated by Louis Berthault in 1812. Bed by François-Honoré Jacob-Desmalter (to Berthault's design?); Beauvais carpet in Savonnerie style. © Arnaudet/RMN, Paris.

Vase, 1806. The painting, by Jacques-François-Joseph Swebach, shows the Château of Saint-Cloud. H 128 cm. Musée du Château de Versailles. © RMN, Paris.
Carpet of the Salon de l'Abdication, Fontainebleau (part of Napoleon's private apartments), by Bellanger, 1809. © Lagiewski/RMN, Paris.

Thrones of the Emperor Napoleon. *Left:* design for the throne and its canopy in the Tuileries Palace, by Charles Percier and Pierre-François-Léonard Fontaine. After a wood-engraving of 1804. © AKG, Paris. *Right:* throne designed by Percier and Fontaine. Musée des Arts Décoratifs, Paris. © Dagli Orti, Paris.

Plate from the Egyptian Service, 1811. Sèvres porcelain. Château de Malmaison et de Bois-Préau. © C. Jean/RMN, Paris. This Sèvres service, commissioned by Vivant Denon and based on engravings from his book, is one of the finest creations inspired by the expedition of the *savants* to Egypt.
Allegorical Portrait of Vivant Denon, by Benjamin Zix. Pen and sepia wash. Musée du Louvre, Paris. © J. Schormans/RMN, Paris.

Designs for cups and saucers from the Dagoty & Honoré factory, first half of the nineteenth century. Watercolour and bodycolour, 51 x 66.7 cm. © Laurent-Sully Jaulmes, Musée des Arts Décoratifs, Paris.

Napoleon's *athénienne*, made by Martin-Guillaume Biennais and Joseph-Gabriel Genu to a design by Charles Percier, 1800–1804. Yew, gilt bronze and silver, H 90 cm. Musée du Louvre, Paris. © Arnaudet/RMN, Paris.
Plate from the *Recueil de décorations intérieures* by Charles Percier and Pierre-François-Léonard Fontaine, 1812. Engraving, coloured in watercolour by B. Schlick. © Laurent-Sully Jaulmes, Musée des Arts Décoratifs, Paris.

Architect's desk, by Jean-Baptiste Youf. Mahogany and mahogany veneer. The desk has openings on both sides, and incorporates a seventeenth-century cabinet with 21 drawers. © Serge Carrié/Galerie Camoin, Paris.
Napoleon's library, Compiègne. Painted ceiling and frieze by the workshop of Dubois and Redouté, 1810. © RMN, Paris.

Secretaire, by Bernard Molitor, c. 1805–10. Mahogany, mahogany veneer, and gilt bronze. © Galerie Bernard Steinitz, Paris.
Armchair, by Pierre-Benoît Marcion, 1809. Mahogany and gilt bronze. Musée National du Château de Fontainebleau. © Lagiewski/RMN, Paris.

The bed of Napoleon as First Consul in the Palais-Royal, Paris, after Charles Percier. From Henry Havard, *Dictionnaire d'ameublement et de décoration* (Quantin, Paris), vol. III, early nineteenth century. © Dagli Orti, Paris.
Clock celebrating the marriage of Napoleon and Marie-Louise, by Pierre-Philippe Thomire, c. 1815. Musée du Louvre, Paris. © RMN, Paris.

The Empress Josephine's bedroom in the Grand Trianon, Versailles. On the right is her dressing table, of ash and gilt bronze, purchased from the merchant Antoine-Thibaut Baudoin in 1809. © Dagli Orti, Paris.
Madame Raymond de Verninac, née Henriette Delacroix (sister of the painter Eugène Delacroix), by Jacques-Louis David. Oil on canvas, 145 x 112 cm. Musée du Louvre, Paris. © RMN, Paris.

Chair with sloping back. Mahogany. Musée des Arts Décoratifs, Paris. © Dagli Orti, Paris.
Plate 12 from the album *Meubles et objets de goût* by Pierre de La Mésangère (1802–35), showing chairs in Consulat style, 1802–4. Bibliothèque des Arts Décoratifs, Paris. © Dagli Orti, Paris.

Two day-beds, by Bernard Molitor. Mahogany and patinated bronze. Their carved ends are decorated with winged griffins copied from antique bas-reliefs, and they rest on bronze lion legs. © Galerie Bernard Steinitz, Paris.
Plate 30 from the album *Meubles et objets de goût* by Pierre de La Mésangère (1802–35), showing beds in Consulat style, 1804. Bibliothèque des Arts Décoratifs, Paris. © Dagli Orti, Paris.

Dressing table, by François-Honoré Jacob-Desmalter, 1808. Mahogany, gilt bronze, and white marble. Musée National du Château de Compiègne. © RMN, Paris.
Madame Récamier (detail), by Jacques-Louis David, begun in 1800 and left unfinished. Oil on canvas, 174 x 244 cm. Musée du Louvre, Paris. © AKG, Paris.

For their help in the preparation of this book, the publishers would like to thank Bernard Baruch Steinitz, G. Dagli Orti, Sonia Edard and Rachel Brishoual of the Union Centrale des Arts Décoratifs, Bernard Garrett and Hervé Mouriacoux of AKG Photo, Paris, Jocelyne Le Brenn of Galerie Camoin Demachy, and Agnès Reboul of the Réunion des Musées Nationaux. The translator, additionally, is grateful for advice on some specific terms to Hubertus Erfurt of Sotheby's, London.